THEODORE ROOSEVELT

The Fight Against Corruption

Written by Jérémy Rocteur
In collaboration with Pierre Frankignoulle
Translated by Jessica Foster

History 50MINUTES.com

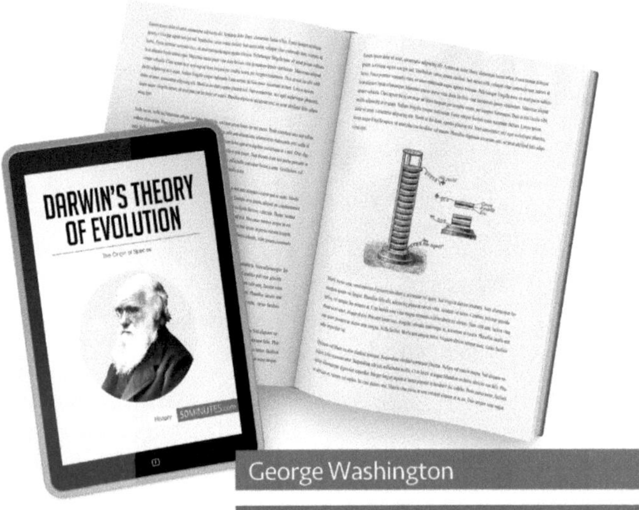

THEODORE ROOSEVELT

KEY INFORMATION

- **Born:** 27 October 1858 in New York.
- **Died:** 6 January 1919 in New York.
- **Political party:** Republican.
- **Dates of election:**
  - 14 September 1901
  - 8 November 1904.
- **Length of term:** seven years.
- **Main achievements:**
  - Modernisation of the presidency
  - Trust regulation
  - Bill on railroad rates
  - Law on monitoring the food and drug industries
  - Making the Navy central to American diplomacy
  - The beginning of benevolent imperialism in the United States.

INTRODUCTION

In 1901, at the age of 42, Theodore Roosevelt became the youngest president in the history of the United States. Full of energy and an excellent public speaker, he was a charismatic leader who never thought twice about disrupting the rules of the presidency. Unlike his predecessor, Roosevelt defended his own political initiatives, readily keeping his distance from his party's ideology. He would do this even more during his second term, which would be one of the most prolific in terms of legislative production in American history.

During his career, he also transformed domestic policy by increasing the number of measures that were part of the Progressive movement. On an international level, he considerably strengthened the role played by his country in the global order of the early 20th century and contributed to the assertion of American imperialism.

A great protector of nature, war hero and defender of the working classes, he remains popular to this day and is considered to be one of the most significant residents of the White House: this is attested by the presence of his effigy next to George Washington (1732-1799), Thomas Jefferson (1743-1826) and Abraham Lincoln (1809-1865) on Mount Rushmore. But the fact that his reputation is intact is also due to his unusual path through life.

BIOGRAPHY

Photograph of Theodore Roosevelt, 1904.

A FRAIL YOUNG MAN WITH AN INCREDIBLE DESTINY

Theodore Roosevelt Jr. was born on 27 October 1858 into a wealthy family. He was the second child of Martha Bullock (1835-1884), who came from a long line of politicians, and Theodore Roosevelt Sr. (1831-1878), an influential man who was close to the then president, Abraham Lincoln. He was affected by congenital problems that made him a frail child. Asthma attacks would mean he would have to fight hard for his health throughout his life.

Despite this handicap, Roosevelt was a dynamic and curious child who threw himself into reading many books of various genres. Being unable to receive a normal education due to his fragile health, he had the advantage of being home-schooled.

During his adolescence, still suffering from his fragility, he decided to start intensive physical training and began boxing. The sport enabled him to strengthen his body and, gradually, he managed to overcome his asthma attacks, which became less frequent.

In 1876, he began studying law at Harvard and became a member of the Republican Party. Although his health was improving, a doctor warned him that he had to lead a quiet life and aim for a sedentary occupation. However, Roosevelt did not heed the doctor's words.

In 1880, he married Alice Hathaway Lee (1861-1884), whom he met at university, but the young woman died four years later in childbirth. The young man's luck was out, as he also lost his mother on that same day. Struggling to cope with his grief, he decided to go to Dakota where he led the life of a cowboy, which taught him a great deal. For several months, he crossed the territory's plains on horseback, built a ranch and divided his time between hunting and writing. He would never really leave behind this way of life. He also took part in the Cuban War of Independence in 1898 as the leader of the 'Rough Riders', the First United States Volunteer Cavalry that he himself founded.

Colonel Roosevelt and the Rough Riders during the Cuban War of Independence.

When he returned to the East Coast in 1886, he got married

for a second time to Edith Kermit Carow (1861-1948), with whom he would have five children and live until he died.

THE FIGHT AGAINST CORRUPTION

Although his family background could have guaranteed him quick progress in his professional career, Roosevelt preferred to start at the bottom and work his way to the top step by step. His interest in politics was so great that he decided to stop his studies to spend all of his time on it. Thanks to his efforts, he was elected three times to the New York State Assembly for year-long terms. This small man, full of enthusiasm and very talkative, soon became the leader of the party's young reformers.

Having been made president of a special committee tasked with investigating the New York City government and council, he acquired a certain reputation among the general public for his fight against corruption. He was assisted in this task by two Democrats and two Republicans who were mostly well-disposed towards him. No service was spared: they found blackmail and extortion in the public prosecutor's office, serious offences in the sheriff's department, buying the silence of policemen, and much more. The evidence was so overwhelming that almost all of his bills aimed at regulating public life in New York were accepted.

During the Republican National Convention in Chicago in June 1884, he did not hesitate before following his instinct and opposing the corrupt, traditional wing of the party who wanted to nominate James Gillespie Blaine (American politician, 1830-1893) as the presidential candidate despite the many suspicions of corruption that weighed upon him, opting to vote instead for George Franklin Edmunds (American politician, 1828-1919), even if he had no chance of winning.

In 1889, he was appointed to the Civil Service Commission, where he served until 1895. He then joined the board of the New York City Police Commissioners for two years. In 1897, he was chosen by President William McKinley (1843-1901) as Assistant Secretary of the Navy, a position he held until 1898, when he left to fight in Cuba.

Crowned with glory, he became Governor of New York upon his return, and held the position from 1898 to 1900. Elected Vice-President in 1901, he took over from William McKinley as President when the latter died. He was elected for a second term in 1904, before handing over to William Howard Taft (1857-1930) in 1909.

DID YOU KNOW?

As well as being a recognised politician, Roosevelt was also a prolific writer and authored around 30 books. He had had this passion since his early childhood, but with age, his writings diversified: his letters were gradually replaced by pamphlets, poems and historical works, among others. His book *The Naval War of 1812* (1882), about America's budding naval power, brought him considerable success and soon became a major work on both sides of the Atlantic.

Following his two terms in office, still drawn to adventure, he continued to travel and notably went to Africa, Asia and South America, where he organised hunts and collected rare animals. He died on 6 January 1919.

POLITICAL, ECONOMIC AND SOCIAL CONTEXT

A GROWING ECONOMY

The end of the 19th century and the beginning of the 20th century were marked by significant economic development. Thanks to steam engines and electricity, production speed increased considerably and most sectors experienced exponential growth. Taking advantage of a cheap workforce, manufacturers managed to amass huge fortunes, helped along by legislation that worked to their advantage, which had been adopted by corrupt politicians.

Additionally, the tendency for financial concentration that had begun in the 1870s increased in the 1880s and 1890s. The number of holdings (financial companies with shares in other firms) exploded and the growing businesses needed capital that only the financial world could grant them. The power of major bankers over the economy therefore grew. Well aware of this, politicians, both Democrat and Republican, began to defend and perpetuate the capitalist system – a system ruled by the oligarchs they belonged to, who could easily be targeted by corruption. However, during both of his terms, Roosevelt tried to change this state of affairs and became the first president to prioritise public interest over private interests.

At the end of the 19th century, however, unbridled growth was brutally stopped in its tracks. At the beginning of 1893, many banks failed and thousands of businesses had to close, thus depriving millions of workers of their salaries. Strikes, which often turned violent, broke out across the country. To manage this situation, the government reflected on the role the United States could play in the world: the solution to the country's economic problems could come from abroad.

OPENING UP TO THE REST OF THE WORLD

In around 1890, the United States became the world's largest economic power, but was still not very visible on the international scene. Indeed, the Monroe Doctrine, adopted in 1823, limited their activity in Europe but still protected the Europeans' colonialist intentions. American foreign policy was therefore largely turned towards Latin America.

However, at the end of the century, American industrial production was so high that internal consumption could no longer absorb it all. They therefore needed to find outlets for it, notably in foreign markets. Several reflections were also made in order to redefine foreign policy in relation to this new state of affairs.

This solution seemed beneficial, as the act of nurturing relationships with potential adversaries would allow the country to channel some of its combative energy elsewhere, while at the same time contributing to the development of a warlike patriotism. Additionally, Britain was struggling to maintain world order, particularly faced with the increasingly powerful German Empire. The idea of American expansionism aimed at neutralising this situation gradually came together: this subsequently paved the way for imperialism. Moreover, the outbreak of the Cuban War of Independence in 1898 offered the perfect pretext for intervening abroad.

THE CUBAN WAR OF INDEPENDENCE

From 1895, Cuban rebels had fought for their independence from Spain. The American president in office at the time, William McKinley, decided to intervene primarily to make access to the South American foreign markets easier and more secure.

After a short campaign, Cuba rejoined the American sphere of influence without becoming an official colony. However, without properly annexing the island, the Americans managed to impose, in the new Cuban constitution, an amendment that authorised them to set up naval bases there, but also "to intervene for the preservation of Cuban independence, the maintenance of a government adequate for the protection of life, property, and individual liberty" (Article 3, Platt Amendment).

In the same year, Congress ratified a treaty to annex Hawaii, and one to annex the Philippines a year later. These events were behind the opposition between:

- The anti-imperialists, such as the writer Mark Twain (1835-1910), who denounced the incompatibility of this annexation with two of the principles of the republic:
  - constitutional (citizens' consent)
  - and moral (pre-eminence of rights over force).

- The expansionists, of whom Roosevelt was one of the main representatives.

However, following the deadly revolts that took place in the Philippines, the first wave of imperialism stopped almost immediately. The Americans therefore only had one option left: peacefully conquer the foreign markets to spread their wealth and investments there. This was the beginning of the Open Door Policy (1898-1900), through which the Americans invoked the right of nationals of any country to travel and do business without facing any discrimination within the areas of influence of other powers.

Gradually, the United States promoted a new world order in which any idea of conquest or colonial domination was irrelevant. However, this was only a façade as, behind the apparently disinterested nature of the tasks that they had set themselves, they were justifying the interventions they could carry out in advance.

AN ANGRY POPULATION

In the second half of the 19th century, the American population grew rapidly. From 1860 to 1900, it increased from 30 to 75 million inhabitants, notably due to the mass influx of immigrants, most of whom came from Central and Southern Europe.

Gradually, the gap between the wealthy and the disadvantaged grew. Factory workers were working in difficult and dangerous conditions. A rebellion was stirring, but strikes were quashed. There was a general sense of discontent, particularly concentrated in the towns. The law and violent repression were no longer sufficient for maintaining order.

However, in order to continue, the system had to be perceived as essential by the most underprivileged strata of society. This is why the myth of the American dream appeared, spread by education, popular literature and even the Church. The message was clear: everyone could hope to become rich if they worked hard. Additionally, millionaires such as Leland Stanford (American politician and business-man, 1824-1893) founded universities, whose primary objec-tive was to educate the officials who would be responsible for maintaining the system (teachers, lawyers, etc.).

However, despite the efforts of the ruling elite, much of pu-blic opinion shared the various criticisms of those in power and nationwide movements emerged.

Mass immigration, which intensified during the final two decades of the 19th century, did nothing to solve the issue as it led to economic competition between the new arrivals and those who had already been there for some time. The workforce became too large, which allowed manufacturers to keep salaries low. The crisis of 1893 and the recession that followed only aggravated the situation: the number of strikes exploded and violence worsened. Some towns saw real worker uprisings. This crisis encouraged politicians to take more Progressive measures.

Progressivism

The term 'progressivism' comes from a collection of movements primarily aimed at emphasising new ideals for American society and adopting legislation that was favourable to progress in society.

This trend was above all a reaction from the public authorities in the face of the discontent of the working classes. But the tacit objective was to counter the rise of socialism, which tended to attract those who felt this sense of discontent. It was therefore a question of bolstering the capitalist system by changing it, and not by implementing radical changes: the leading classes wanted above all to calm the social climate. The reform process further accelerated in 1907, a year in which socialists and trade unions considerably increased their influence.

It was in this extremely turbulent context that Roosevelt entered the White House.

HIGHLIGHTS

THE DEFENCE OF WORKERS' RIGHTS

When he arrived in the Oval Office following William McKinley's death, Roosevelt announced that he did not want to change his predecessor's policies. However, motivated by the desire to create a fairer and more egalitarian society, he proved that he was ready to defend his political ideas.

In his opinion, most of the economic and social problems that the United States was experiencing in the early 20th century required more centralisation and intervention on the part of the federal government. During his time as Governor of New York, he had already taken measures aimed at improving life for the working classes. In favour of increased regulation of businesses, he attacked difficult working conditions and notably obtained:

- a reduction in the working hours of women and children
- 38-hour weeks for State employees.

When he became President of the United States, Roosevelt did not give up this fight and continually tried to impose federal checks on private businesses in order to limit the abuses they were committing to the detriment of American citizens.

He also readily intervened in disagreements between employers and workers, the first instance of this being in 1902. At the end of the year, several coal mines were non-functional due to strikes. Fearing a shortage in winter, Roosevelt threatened to send in the army to quash the revolt. Faced with this pressure, the managers of the mines agreed to the establishment of an independent negotiation committee, which the president ensured swayed in favour of the miners.

Photograph of the committee appointed to resolve the coal miners' dispute.

TRUST REGULATION

The power of businesses at that time was so great that most Americans were worried about being forced to bow to the decisions of industry investors. Aware of the problem but also of the importance of trusts (powerful businesses, often with a monopoly and therefore an influence over the economy) in the 20th-century economy, Roosevelt sought to regulate them rather than dissolve them.

Consequently, he rejected Thomas Jefferson's legacy of limited government intervention, although this was an idea that was shared by most of his predecessors. To reach his objective, Roosevelt wanted to create a government administration made up of experts whose entire role would be to regulate all the corporations trading between different states. Thus the Bureau of Corporations was set up; its mission was to monitor salaries in limited companies. Additionally, this new federal agency allowed the president to shape public opinion and to put forward bills on regulation to Congress.

With the support of the Supreme Court, he took legal action against a railroad holding company in which the largest financial names of the time could be found, and even ordered its dissolution. He thus sought to show his independence from the business world and hoped that the threat of dissolution would encourage business leaders to accept his regulation measures. He then challenged other companies and, within two years, 42 suits had been brought, giving Roosevelt his reputation as the 'trust-buster'.

RAILROAD REGULATION

The president's second hobby horse was the regulation of the railroad companies engaged in interstate commerce, many of whom were indulging in abusive practices. Having learned that some companies were using private freight carriages to transport goods for honoured senders, Roosevelt demanded that fixed rates be set, whoever the sender, to avoid any discrimination against small carriers.

However, while regulation was supported by most citizens, some people feared that this decision would mean a general increase in living costs following increased railroad rates, especially at a time when inflation was surging. Despite this common fear, after a struggle that lasted several years, the president managed to get the Hepburn Act passed in 1906. Thanks to this legislation, the federal government could now set rates and investigate the accounts of private companies involved in interstate commerce.

HEALTHCARE LAWS AND NATURE CONSERVATION

During his term, Roosevelt also decided to tackle public health, which had not been regulated much previously. Informed of the disastrous hygiene conditions in the country's abattoirs, he was behind the Meat Inspection Act, passed in 1906, which guaranteed inspections of the food industry. The purity of food and pharmaceutical products was also guaranteed by the Pure Food and Drug Act, passed in the same year.

A great nature enthusiast, Roosevelt also worked on laws on conservation. He fought for a more rational use of natural resources and took important measures to conserve forests and nature sites. Among these measures was the declaration of many locations, including the Grand Canyon, as national parks.

A GROWING PLACE ON THE INTERNATIONAL SCENE

In terms of foreign policy, Roosevelt tried to make his country more visible on the international scene. He sought to meet two objectives:

- to reinforce American hegemony across the continent
- and to make his country indispensable in the Atlantic and the Pacific.

The president promoted global stability through what was known as a balance of power. In this way, the ideology of benevolent American imperialism began: while defending the United States' interests, this encouraged peace and stability in the world. He did not, however, rule out recourse to military force to promote the interests of his country that seemed legitimate to him, and maintained a hegemonic attitude towards Latin America.

This ambitious diplomacy strategy depended on:

- The 'Big Stick' strategy, embodied by the US Navy, who were above all a dissuasive force to guarantee peace: this also overlapped with military 'preparedness', which demanded that the armed forces be permanently ready for war;

- Active diplomacy in every continent thanks to presidential mediation in several conflicts.

The United States therefore had a powerful navy, which Roosevelt had worked on throughout his career. As Assistant Secretary of the Navy, he considerably improved the department's efficiency and helped to transform the Navy into a force that was no longer defensive, but offensive, and able to carry out missions several hundred miles away from its home ports. During his presidency, Roosevelt continued this effort, aiming to improve naval tactics through technology and better administration. Additionally, wanting to ensure that the Navy was led by a strong power, he handed over its control from Congress to the president himself.

Roosevelt addresses officers and crewmen on the ship *Connecticut* from atop one of its gun turrets.

Furthermore, he was convinced that the Atlantic and the Pacific had to be linked by a canal that would be controlled solely by the Americans. This would guarantee them not just trading benefits, but also a better distribution of their fleet. To manage this, he became involved in a war in Latin America, by encouraging the subversive revolution of Panama State against Colombia. Once Panama had gained its independence, Roosevelt could now go ahead with his plan and ratified a treaty with the new state on 18 November 1903, guaranteeing the United States permanent use, control and occupation of Panama, under the pretext of guarding its independence.

THE NOBEL PEACE PRIZE

Roosevelt supported the creation and reinforcement of international institutions to guarantee global stability. He was also convinced that the United States' newly-acquired power meant that they had a duty to promote peace, even if American interests were not directly affected. His presidency was thus behind many mediation treaties, par-ticularly during the Russo-Japanese War (1904-1905), during which the president intervened as a mediator to put an end to the conflict and thus preserve the balance of power, which earned him the Nobel Peace Prize in 1906.

Considering Japan to be one of the 'superior' nations, he agreed to recognise its sovereignty over Korea, in exchange for silence over potential aggressive American operations in the Philippines, a country subject to frequent turmoil. Finally, in 1907, an agreement was signed with Japan which recognised its supremacy over Manchuria (Northeast China) in exchange for the reassertion of the status quo in the Pacific and of the Open Door Policy in China.

THE RUSSO-JAPANESE WAR

After the restoration of the Emperor in 1867, Japan wanted to compete with Western powers. To do this, it began an intensive industrialisation process and created a modern army with the aim of expanding across Asia. After a series of successful operations, Japanese expansion was stopped by several Western countries, including Russia, which staked claims on the same territories as Japan (Korea, Manchuria and Northeast China).

Eager to seek revenge, Japan launched a surprise attack on the Russian fleet on 9 February 1904. On 27 May 1905, during the naval Battle of Tsushima, the Russian fleet in the Baltic Sea was completely destroyed. Russia had not only been defeated, but humiliated.

Wary of Japanese claims in the Pacific, which could soon threaten American interests, Roosevelt offered the mediation of the United States. Thanks to his insight, he managed to put a stop to the Russo-Japanese War and satisfy both sides: Russia would not pay any compensation, but would concede territory to Japan and withdraw any claims to Manchuria and Korea.

THE 1912 PRESIDENTIAL CAMPAIGN

In 1910, the Republican Party split into two groups: the conservatives, including Roosevelt's successor, William Howard Taft, and the Progressives. Realising that his political legacy was under threat, Roosevelt decided to come back to the political scene three years after withdrawing from public life. Additionally, many of the party's Progressives were saying that they wanted him to be their candidate in the next elections. After hesitating for some time, he agreed to start a new campaign, but did not receive the Republican Party's nomination, which was in the hands of the conservatives.

He therefore decided to create a new party, the Progressive Party, and to be its candidate. Following Roosevelt's main ideas, the party defended:

- the permanent monitoring of companies in interstate commerce
- health insurance and social insurance for the unemployed and the elderly
- women's right to vote.

Roosevelt campaigning for president in 1912.

Although he was not re-elected, Roosevelt won over a quarter of the votes, an unmatched amount for a third party. Coming in second place, he finished ahead of the Republican candidate, William Howard Taft, but had to concede victory to the Democrat Thomas Woodrow Wilson (1856-1924).

IMPACT

AN IMPROVEMENT IN QUALITY OF LIFE

The determination that Roosevelt showed throughout his career allowed him to impose federal intervention in several areas that were important to the population: public health, the right to work, trust regulation, etc. Living conditions therefore considerably improved during his presidency. Proof of this was the increase in average age from 49 in 1901 to 56 in 1920.

He is also recognised as one of the precursors to modern ecology due to his intervention for the protection of forests. Through his various actions, he managed to increase the areas of federal reservation fivefold.

BOLSTERING THE ROLE OF PRESIDENT

Aware of the power of the press, Roosevelt transformed journalists into assistants of executive power. Allowing the media to produce pithy articles about his latest de-clarations, he took over the news by ensuring that he was always on the front page of the papers. He also laid the groundwork for presidential press conferences, something his successor would establish as an institution. Thanks to this strengthening of the executive and of federal power, the president could now fight more effectively against the excesses of liberalism.

A PROGRESSIVE DOMESTIC POLICY?

While his activities were generally viewed in a positive light, Roosevelt's action against trusts was subject to debate. Roosevelt had quickly been nicknamed the 'trust-buster', although his main objective was not to dissolve them but rather to regulate them.

Despite claiming to be Progressive, Roosevelt was actually much more conservative than many people imagine. Most of his advisers had come from the industrial and financial worlds, and the government measures he adopted did not weaken their major interests, but strengthened them. The smallest businesses were in fact unable to respect the new, much more demanding standards. Finally, the sanctions provided for by this legislation were not applied in reality.

However, by strengthening the executive and introducing many government regulations, he reminded everyone that power resided in Washington and not Wall Street. He therefore helped to re-establish the balance between public power and private interests.

Thanks to everything he did for the middle classes, he also managed to channel popular discontent and make government administration more efficient without seriously damaging the private economy. The United States therefore enjoyed renewed growth and prosperity.

THE UNITED STATES' SELF-ASSERTION ON THE GLOBAL SCENE

Roosevelt also helped to make his country more visible on an international level. To do this, he mostly had recourse to the development of the Navy, thanks to his Big Stick strategy. Thus, the Navy's size and ability increased in each year of his presidency.

Cartoon depicting Roosevelt's Big Stick ideology, 1904.

Eager to give his country a more active role in global affairs, he took part in the theorisation and assertion of the United States' benevolent imperialism: they did not think twice about defending and imposing their own interests while promoting an ideology of peace and global stability. He also gave his country a reputation as a mediating power, as was the case during the Russo-Japanese War.

SUMMARY

1858
27th Oct.: Birth of Theodore Roosevelt

1882
First activity on the political scene

1901
2nd Sept.: Big Stick policy
**14th Sept.: Elected 26th President
of the United States**

1903
18th Nov.: Acquisition of transit and intervention
rights over the Panama Canal

1905
4th Mar.: Second election

1906
10th Dec.: Awarded the Nobel Peace Prize

1908
The Grand Canyon becomes a national park

1909
4th Mar.: **Election of William Howard Taft**

1919
6th Jan.: Death of Theodore Roosevelt

- Theodore Roosevelt was from a wealthy family, but his fragile health did not set him up for an extraordinary fate. However, as he was full of energy and drive, and very talkative, he eventually overcame his health problems and reached the highest political office in America.
- He entered politics while he was still very young, and was elected several times to the New York State Assembly, where he quickly gained a reputation as an enemy of corruption and established himself as the leader of the young reformers of the Republican Party.
- Devastated by the death of his first wife, who died in childbirth, he went to live as a cowboy on the plains of Dakota, dividing his time between hunting and writing. This experience taught him the importance of nature and its conservation.
- During the Cuban War of Independence in 1898, he joined as a volunteer soldier and came back crowned with glory.
- Appointed in 1901 to the position of Vice-President to William McKinley, he succeeded him in the same year following his assassination and, at the age of 42, became the youngest ever US President. He was elected in November 1904 for a second term.
- A great nature enthusiast, Roosevelt also worked on conservation laws. He thus took important measures to conserve forests and natural sites.
- Taking advantage of a strengthened federal administration, he fought against the excesses of liberalism. He took measures for increased trust regulation, which benefited the working classes as well as American consumers.
- On an international level, Roosevelt reinforced the United States' position, making them a major power

thanks to a diplomacy that was essentially based on new American naval power.

- After he left the White House, he continued to occupy a central role on the American political scene, relentlessly fighting to defend his ideas.
- For his heroism as a soldier and his fight for workers and environmental protection, he is now considered to have been one of the most important residents of the White House.

We want to hear from you!
Leave a comment on your online library
and share your favourite books on social media!

BIBLIOGRAPHY

- Arnold, P. (2009) *Remaking the Presidency*. Lawrence: University Press of Kansas.
- Carnes, M. and Garraty, J. (1999) *American National Biography*. Oxford: Oxford University Press.
- Cashman, S. D. (1998) *America Ascendant: From Theodore Roosevelt to FDR in the Century of American Power, 1901-1945*. New York: New York University Press.
- Cooper, J. M. (1990) *Pivotal Decades: the United States, 1900-1920*. London: W. W. Norton.
- Morris, E. (1979) *The Rise of Theodore Roosevelt*. New York: Coward, McCann & Geoghegan.
- Morris, E. (2001) *Theodore Rex*. New York: Random House.
- Morris, E. (2011) *Colonel Roosevelt*. New York: Random House.
- Ricard, S. (1991) *Theodore Roosevelt: Principes et pratique d'une politique étrangère*. Marseilles: Université de Provence.
- Ricard, S. (2011) *A Companion to Theodore Roosevelt*. Malden: Blackwell Publishing.
- Watts, S. (2006) *Rough Rider in the White House: Theodore Roosevelt and the Politics of Desire*. Chicago: University of Chicago Press.

ADDITIONAL SOURCES

- Diner, S. (1998) *A Very Different Age: Americans of the Progressive Era*. New York: Hill and Wang.
- Edwards, R. (2006) *New Spirits: Americans in the Gilded Age, 1865-1905*. Oxford: Oxford University Press.
- Jones, G. (2013) *Honor in the Dust. Theodore Roosevelt, War in the Philippines, and the Rise and Fall of America's Imperial Dream*. New York: New American Library.

ICONOGRAPHIC SOURCES

- Photograph of Theodore Roosevelt, 1904. © Library of Congress.
- Colonel Roosevelt and the Rough Riders during the Cuban War of Independence. Royalty-free reproduction picture.
- Photograph of the committee appointed to resolve the coal miners' dispute. © Library of Congress.
- Roosevelt addresses officers and crewmen on the ship *Connecticut* from atop one of its gun turrets. © Naval History and Heritage Command.
- Roosevelt campaigning for president in 1912. Royalty-free reproduction picture.
- Cartoon depicting Roosevelt's Big Stick ideology, 1904. Royalty-free reproduction picture.

IMPROVE YOUR GENERAL KNOWLEDGE

IN A BLINK OF AN EYE !

www.50minutes.com